BRITISH RAILWAYS STEAMING FROM ST. PANCRAS TO ST. ENOCH

Compiled by

PETER HANDS & COLIN RICHARDS

DEFIANT PUBLICATIONS
190 Yoxall Road,
Shirley, Solihull,
West Midlands.

Printed on behalf of Richard Netherwood Ltd. by Gorenjski Tisk, Slovenia

CURRENT STEAM PHOTOGRAPH ALBUMS AVAILABLE
FROM DEFIANT PUBLICATIONS

VOLUME 1
A4 size - Hardback. 100 pages -180 b/w photographs.
£8.95 + £1.00 postage.
ISBN 0 946857 12 1.

VOLUME 2
A4 size - Hardback. 100 pages -180 b/w photographs.
£8.95 + £1.00 postage.
ISBN 0 946857 13 X.

VOLUME 13
A4 size - Hardback. 100 pages -182 b/w photographs.
£11.95 + £1.00 postage.
ISBN 0 946857 33 4.

VOLUME 4
A4 size - Hardback. 100 pages -180 b/w photographs.
£9.95 + £1.00 postage.
ISBN 0 946857 17 2.

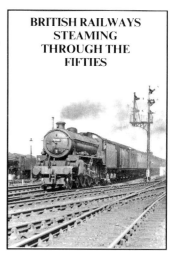

VOLUME 5
A4 size - Hardback. 100 pages -180 b/w photographs.
£9.95 + £1.00 postage.
ISBN 0 946857 22 9.

VOLUME 6
A4 size - Hardback. 100 pages -180 b/w photographs.
£9.95 + £1.00 postage.
ISBN 0 946857 23 7.

VOLUME 7
A4 size - Hardback. 100 pages -180 b/w photographs.
£11.95 + £1.00 postage.
ISBN 0 946857 31 8.

VOLUME 8
A4 size - Hardback. 100 pages -180 b/w photographs.
£11.95 + £1.00 postage.
ISBN 0 946857 32 6.

BRITISH RAILWAYS
STEAMING
THROUGH THE
FIFTIES

IN
PREPARATION

BRITISH RAILWAYS
STEAMING
THROUGH THE
FIFTIES

IN
PREPARATION

BRITISH RAILWAYS
STEAMING ON
THE EX-LNER
LINES

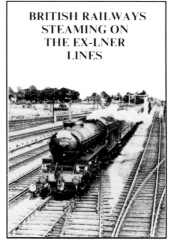

BRITISH RAILWAYS
STEAMING
FROM ST. PANCRAS
TO ST. ENOCH

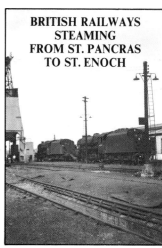

VOLUME 9

VOLUME 10

VOLUME 2
A4 size - Hardback. 100 pages -187 b/w photographs.
£11.95 + £1.00 postage.
ISBN 0 946857 34 2.

A4 size - Hardback. 96 pages -173 b/w photographs.
£12.95 + £1.00 postage.
ISBN 0 946857 36 9.

CURRENT STEAM PHOTOGRAPH ALBUMS AVAILABLE
FROM DEFIANT PUBLICATIONS

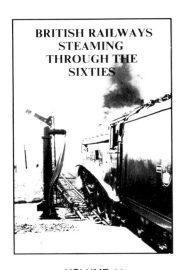

BRITISH RAILWAYS STEAMING THROUGH THE SIXTIES

VOLUME 11
A4 size - Hardback. 100 pages
-180 b/w photographs.
£10.95 + £1.00 postage.
ISBN 0 946857 24 5.

BRITISH RAILWAYS STEAMING THROUGH THE SIXTIES

VOLUME 12
A4 size - Hardback. 100 pages
-182 b/w photographs.
£11.95 + £1.00 postage.
ISBN 0 946857 27 X.

BRITISH RAILWAYS STEAMING THROUGH THE SIXTIES

VOLUME 13

IN PREPARATION
APRIL 1991

BRITISH RAILWAYS STEAMING THROUGH PETERBOROUGH

A4 size - Hardback. 100 pages
-163 b/w photographs.
£10.95 + £1.00 postage.
ISBN 0 946857 26 1.

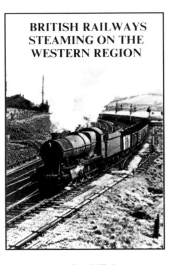

BRITISH RAILWAYS STEAMING ON THE WESTERN REGION

VOLUME 3
A4 size - Hardback. 100 pages
-179 b/w photographs.
£10.95 + £1.00 postage.
ISBN 0 946857 25 3.

BRITISH RAILWAYS STEAMING ON THE WESTERN REGION

IN PREPARATION

VOLUME 4

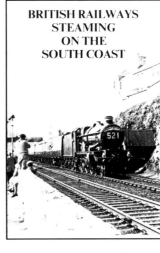

BRITISH RAILWAYS STEAMING ON THE SOUTH COAST

A4 size - Hardback. 100 pages
-182 b/w photographs.
£11.95 + £1.00 postage.
ISBN 0 946857 29 6.

BRITISH RAILWAYS STEAMING ON THE SOUTHERN REGION

IN PREPARATION

VOLUME 3

BRITISH RAILWAYS STEAMING ON THE LONDON MIDLAND REGION

VOLUME 3
A4 size - Hardback. 100 pages
-181 b/w photographs.
£11.95 + £1.00 postage.
ISBN 0 946857 28 8.

BRITISH RAILWAYS STEAMING ON THE LONDON MIDLAND REGION

IN PREPARATION

VOLUME 4

BRITISH RAILWAYS STEAMING ON THE EX-LNER LINES

VOLUME 2

IN PREPARATION
APRIL 1991

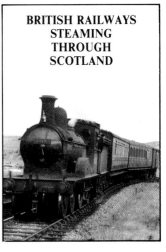

BRITISH RAILWAYS STEAMING THROUGH SCOTLAND

VOLUME 1
A4 size - Hardback. 96 pages
-180 b/w photographs.
£12.95 + £1.00 postage.
ISBN 0 946857 35 0.

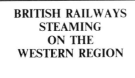

ACKNOWLEDGEMENTS

Grateful thanks are extended to the following contributors of photographs not only for their use in this book, but for their kind patience and long term loan of negatives/ photographs whilst this book was being compiled.

T.R.AMOS TAMWORTH	H.H.BLEADS BIRMINGHAM	W.G.BOYDEN BEXHILL*
B.W.L.BROOKSBANK LONDON	N.L.BROWNE ALDERSHOT	R.BUTTERFIELD MIRFIELD
R.S.CARPENTER BIRMINGHAM	J.K.CARTER MILLHOLME	K.ELLIS SWINDON
A.N.H.GLOVER BIRMINGHAM	J.D.GOMERSALL SHEFFIELD	PETER HAY HOVE
R.HENNEFER SUTTON COLDFIELD	M.F.HIGSON THE SMOKEBOX	R.W.HINTON GLOUCESTER
H.L.HOLLAND ST.CATHERINES, ONTARIO, CANADA CHEAM		F.HORNBY NORTH CHEAM
C.HUGHES AMESBURY	A.C.INGRAM WISBECH	H.N.JAMES IPSWICH
D.K.JONES MOUNTAIN ASH	B.J.MILLER BARRY	T.B.OWEN *
W.G.PIGGOTT UNKNOWN	A.J.PIKE *	STUART PITCHFORTH SANDAL
N.E.PREEDY HUCCLECOTE	B.RANDS WESTON-SUPER-MARE	J.SCHATZ LITTLETHORPE
K.L.SEAL ANDOVERSFORD	G.W.SHARPE BARNSLEY	DEREK SINGLETON **
M.S.STOKES MARPLE	J.M.TOLSON *	MIKE TURNER BROAD HINTON
D.WEBSTER ***		

* Courtesy of the Frank Hornby collection.
** From the Preston Whiteley collection (Kendall) courtesy of David Alexander.
*** Courtesy of the Norman Preedy collection.

Front Cover - A view of part of the shed yard at 14B Cricklewood on 23rd August 1964, a few months before the depot closed to steam. Nearest the camera is LMS Class 5 4-6-0 No 44717, from 16B Annesley on the former Great Central main line. In front of No 44717 is LMS Class 8F 2-8-0 No 48704, another visitor to Cricklewood - from 15C Kettering. (J.K.Carter)

ISBN 0 946857 36 9

(C) P.B.HANDS/C.RICHARDS 1991
FIRST PUBLISHED 1991

INTRODUCTION

The appearance of BRITISH RAILWAYS STEAMING FROM ST.PANCRAS TO ST.ENOCH is in response to requests by a number of regular readers of the 'BR Steaming' series of albums. In the main we follow the old 'Midland' routes from London to Carlisle and the former 'Glasgow & South Western' line between Dumfries and Glasgow.

The authors have attempted to vary the locations and types of locomotive classes within the pages of this album in order to please the varied interests of our readers. Some areas of greater interest, such as Carlisle, Derby, Leeds, Leicester, Nottingham, Sheffield, St.Enoch and St.Pancras have been given more coverage than others.

The 'BR Steaming' series of books are designed to give the ordinary, everyday steam photographic enthusiast of the 1950's and 1960's a chance to participate in and give pleasure to others whilst recapturing the twilight days of steam.

Apart from the 1950's and 1960's series, individual albums like this one will be produced from time to time. Wherever possible, no famous names will be found nor will photographs which have been published before be used. Nevertheless, the content and quality of the majority of photographs used will be second to none.

The majority of the photographs used in this album have been contributed by readers of Peter Hands series of booklets entitled 'What Happened to Steam' & 'BR Steam Shed Allocations' and from readers of the earlier 'BR Steaming Through the Sixties' albums. In normal circumstances these may have been hidden from the public eye for ever.

The continuation of the 'BR Steaming' series etc., depends upon you the reader. If you feel you have suitable material of BR steam locomotives between 1948-1968 and wish to contribute them towards the series and other future publications please contact either:

Peter Hands,
190 Yoxall Road,   OR
Shirley, Solihull,
West Midlands B90 3RN

Colin Richards,
28 Kendrick Close,
Damson Parkway, Solihull,
West Midlands B92 0QD

CONTENTS

1) The magnificent overall roof looks down upon the now listed station at St.Pancras where we begin our long sojourn to St.Enoch. There is steam and smoke a'plenty as highly polished BR *Britannia* Class 4-6-2 No 70052 *Firth of Tay*, from 5A Crewe (North), makes ready for departure with a Locomotive Club of Great Britain special on 24th April 1965. (D.Webster collection - courtesy of N.E.Preedy)

2) From this 1964 angle we have a fine view of the overall roof and the immediate approaches to St.Pancras station, which includes the main signalbox. LMS Class 5 4-6-0 No 45144, a 14A Cricklewood locomotive, belches out black smoke as it accelerates a boat train to Tilbury out of the terminus. Time was not on the side of No 45144 which was to be transferred to 16C Derby in June 1964 and condemned the same month. (Peter Hay)

3) The peace and quiet within the cavernous confines of the arched roof at St.Pancras is shattered by the noise of the steam escaping from the safety valves of LMS *Royal Scot* Class 4-6-0 No 46140 *The King's Royal Rifle Corps,* a resident of 14B Kentish Town, as it waits to leave with a northbound Manchester express on a gloomy day in 1961. No 46140 was destined to be one of the last working survivors of the class. (D.Webster collection - courtesy of N.E.Preedy)

4) The main fleet of named passenger locomotives which worked the former Midland Main Line from St.Pancras were the LMS *Jubilee* Class 4-6-0's. One of their number, based at 55A Leeds (Holbeck), No 45564 *New South Wales,* departs with a Bradford express on 31st March 1956, under the watchful observation of two soot-encrusted upper semaphore signals. (N.L.Browne)

5) Double-heading of expresses to and from St.Pancras was a common feature during the days of steam. A group of spotters, in the dress of the day, note the arrival of LMS Class 2P 4-4-0 No 40420, from 14B Kentish Town (bereft of shedplate), as it pilots LMS *Jubilee* Class 4-6-0 No 45627 *Sierra Leone* (16A Nottingham) on 3rd May 1958. No 40420 is just six months away from withdrawal, eventually being cut up at Doncaster in August 1960. (D.K.Jones)

6) The main passenger depot associated with St.Pancras was at 14B Kentish Town which became a rather forlorn looking place prior to complete closure around April 1963. 41C Millhouses allocated LMS *Royal Scot* Class 4-6-0 No 46147 *The Northamptonshire Regiment* has its wheel arrangement reduced to 4-4-0 due to a pair of drivers having been removed for attention of some kind on 5th October 1961. (N.L.Browne)

7) A rather bedraggled LMS Hughes Class 6P5F 'Crab' 2-6-0 No 42931 puts in an appearance in the shed yard at Kentish Town, being a visitor from the not too distant shed at 1A Willesden on 5th May 1960. A month later and No 42931 found itself at a new home in a more pleasant environment at 24J Lancaster (Green Ayre). (N.L.Browne)

8) Much of the work associated with the suburban services in and out of St.Pancras was carried out by the erstwhile Fowler designed LMS Class 3 2-6-2 Tanks until the diesel multiple units arrived and then their ranks were decimated rather rapidly until all examples had disappeared from 14B Kentish Town by August 1962. No 40022 is photographed for posterity out of steam in a roundhouse on 8th October 1961. (N.L.Browne)

9) In its heyday Kentish Town boasted three roundhouses and a compact yard, east of the main line to the north of the station, but not much of the shed could be seen from the running lines, always frustrating for spotters. In the yard on 8th October 1961 is LMS Class 3F 'Jinty' 0-6-0T No 47437 with a chalked smokebox number. (N.L.Browne)

10) 14A Cricklewood was the principal freight depot for Midland line services to and from London and it presumably took over the remaining steam passenger turns after the closure of Kentish Town. Posing for the camera in bright sunshine on 7th June 1959 is BR Class 9F 2-10-0 No 92127, a type based in large numbers at 15A Wellingborough. At this point in time No 92127 was just over two years old. (A.N.H.Glover)

11) Many of the excellent LMS *Royal Scot* Class 4-6-0's found themselves at more obscure depots, on more menial tasks once they had been ousted by diesel power from sheds on the West Coast Main Line, such as No 46143 *The South Staffordshire Regiment*, from 16D Annesley on the former Great Central Main Line. Minus shedplate it stands in the yard at Cricklewood on 26th May 1963 a few months before condemnation. (T.R.Amos)

12) Like Kentish Town, Cricklewood had a number of Fowler LMS Class 3 2-6-2 Tanks on its books for use on local passenger services. No 39, later 40039, is parked adjacent to the back of several large poster hoardings in Cricklewood yard on 5th June 1948. This engine, fitted with condensing equipment for use on the Moorgate line, is a visitor on this day from 14C St.Albans. (T.B.Owen)

13) One of the massive LMS Beyer-Garrett Class 2-6-6-2 Tanks No 47995, from 18A Toton, is in the twilight of its career on 8th April 1956, as can be seen by its rather shoddy condition, as it puts in an appearance at Cricklewood. It was taken out of service in July 1957 and scrapped at Crewe Works the same month. 14A, which changed code to 14B on 9th September 1963 died, as a steam depot, on 14th December 1964. (N.L.Browne)

14) An elderly Johnson Midland Railway designed (later LMS) Class 4P 'Compound' 4-4-0 No 41091, from 15D Bedford, passes Cricklewood carriage sidings and a freight being headed by an unidentified LMS Class 3F 0-6-0T on its way into London St.Pancras with a lengthy up local passenger train on 23rd September 1950. A few years on and the writing was on the wall for many former Midland Railway types, like No 41091. (B.W.L.Brooksbank)

15) We move away from the heart of London and head out into the suburbs. LMS Class 5 4-6-0 No 45056, allocated to 19B Millhouses, tracks northwards through Mill Hill Broadway station, between Hendon and Elstree, with milk empties bound for Carlisle from Cricklewood, on 3rd October 1953. Both members of the footplate crew lean out of the cab of their charge in an effort to be properly recorded on film. (R.Butterfield)

16) The countryside to the north of Radlett is the setting for this photograph of LMS Class 3 2-6-2T No 40022, from 14C St.Albans and fitted with condensing apparatus, as it steams along with the 5.20 pm local passenger from St.Pancras to St.Albans on 30th August 1958. When St.Albans shed closed in early 1960, No 40022 rotated between 14B Kentish Town and 14A Cricklewood sheds before being withdrawn in December 1962. (B.W.L.Brooksbank)

17) On what is presumably a Bank Holiday period, 30th August 1958, BR Class 9F 2-10-0 No 92019, a 15A Wellingborough engine, heads southwards towards London near to Napsbury, the next station northbound from Radlett, with an empty stock working. No 92019 remained at Midland orientated sheds until June 1964 when it was reallocated to its final base at 12A Carlisle (Kingmoor) from 15C Kettering. (B.W.L.Brooksbank)

18) This particular photographer was rather busy around the St.Albans area on 30th August 1958 as this third picture in a row testifies to. He has moved up the line to a location to the south of St.Albans City station where he records LMS Class 5 4-6-0 No 45253, based at 16A Nottingham where it had been transferred to in October 1957 from 14B Kentish Town, as it speeds towards him with the 10.40 am Bradford - St.Pancras. (B.W.L.Brooksbank)

19) A frail looking goods shed in the background offers scant protection to the assortment of fitted wagons it harbours on 1st August 1959. In the foreground LMS Class 8F 2-8-0 No 48385, yet another 15A Wellingborough locomotive, scuttles past the camera light engine and heads northbound through Luton station. No 48385 remained at Wellingborough shed until a transfer in January 1963 took it to 2F Woodford Halse. (N.L.Browne)

20) The 1st August 1959 was a gloomy day, devoid of any sunshine, when Fairburn LMS Class 4 2-6-4T No 42156 (14B Kentish Town) arrived with a Luton only relief local from St.Pancras at the end of its journey. With the signals behind No 42156 showing STOP, it appears that the signalman in the box in the right of this frame has been somewhat premature in replacing his levers before the whole of the train has cleared the section. (N.L.Browne)

21) Moving five days on in time, to 6th June 1959, the weather certainly had not improved, if anything it had worsened, judging by the heavy clouds. With steam to spare, BR Crosti-boilered Class 9F 2-10-0 No 92024 (15A Wellingborough) eases its way past a platform which is being newly constructed at Luton, with a southbound mineral train. (N.L.Browne)

22) As we continue our journey we halt briefly at Bedford for a glimpse of both the station and shed. An upper quadrant signal stands sentinel like, guarding the barrow crossing on 31st July 1951, as LMS Class 5 4-6-0 No 44661, from 17A Derby, arrives with an unidentified express. In its latter years of life No 44661 served from a host of sheds, including a lengthy spell on the North Wales main line. (H.N.James)

23) The Derby designed BR Class 2 2-6-2 Tanks were nowhere as near as popular as the Class 3 and Class 4 counterparts and had relatively short working lives. Black smoke drifts upwards from an almost new example of the class, No 84005, based at the near-at-hand shed in 1955. This particular engine was subjected to a spate of transfers during its working life, mostly on the Midland Division, before withdrawal in November 1965. (G.W.Sharpe)

24) A longstanding favourite of the local shed at Bedford was former Midland Railway Class 3F 0-6-0 No 43428, which was based there for many years. It is seen here in the yard, in a rather less than well maintained condition, in June 1962, posing over an ash disposal road. The concrete coaling plant can just be observed, towering over the small, four road shed. (Peter Hay)

25) Brighton inspired BR Class 4 2-6-4T No 80061 takes a rest in the yard at Bedford, in company with BR Class 2 2-6-2T No 84005, on an unspecified day in October 1954. The former engine ended its days working from sheds in Scotland, being taken out of service from 66A Polmadie (Glasgow) in December 1966. Bedford shed, 15D, was recoded twice before closure in September 1963, to 14E (April 1958) and 14C (September 1963). (A.N.H.Glover)

26) An overcast day helps to keep steam close to the ground as can be seen in this picture taken on 27th February 1965. The chimney of a filthy BR Class 9F 2-10-0 No 92123, from 15A Leicester (Midland), is obscured by the same as it heads a partially fitted freight near to Oakley station, which is photographed from the carriage of an express. Oakley, situated between Bedford and Wellingborough, closed in 1958. (N.E.Preedy)

27) Having already 'spotted' a number of locomotives from Wellingborough shed it is only fair to briefly pause at the depot which once had two separate roundhouses, prior to 1964 when one was demolished to clear the way for a diesel depot. In front of one roundhouse, on 10th July 1960, is BR Class 9F 2-10-0 No 92054, a local inhabitant of the depot, eventually withdrawn from 8C Speke Junction in May 1968. (W.G.Boyden)

18

28) Shed Masters were not normally associated with 'acts of friendliness' when it came to shed visits, official or unofficial. Here, however, one is captured on film (a rare event) posing in front of a BR Franco-Crosti Class 9F 2-10-0 No 92025 on a brightly lit day in August 1955. Like many sheds, Wellingborough also changed shedcodes, from 15A to 15B in September 1963. It closed to steam in June 1966. (A.J.Pike)

29) Words fail, as to how one can describe the external condition of 15A Leicester (Midland) based BR Class 2 2-6-0 No 78027, in steam in the shed yard at 15C Kettering on 27th February 1965. This shed, of Midland Railway vintage, is only four months away from complete closure, whilst the fate of No 78027 fares little better, being made surplus to requirements three months further on. (D.Webster collection - courtesy of N.E.Preedy)

30) The dead line at Kettering shed on 18th November 1962, coded 15B at this date in time, hosts the rusting hulk of one of its former working inmates. Many locomotives, upon withdrawal, were cut up almost straight away. Others, like former Midland Railway Class 3F 0-6-0 No 43249 lingered on for months and years. Condemned in December 1959, No 43249 was stored at Kettering for four years being cut up at Derby Works in December 1962. (T.R.Amos)

31) Cleanliness was obviously not the order of the day in the Leicester area in February 1965. Observed by its footplate crew on 27th of this month, BR Class 9F 2-10-0 No 92122, a 15A Leicester (Midland) engine, is noted in steam on the turntable at Kettering. This locomotive still had a future once Leicester shed decided it was of no further use, by being transferred to 8H Birkenhead in April 1965. (D.Webster collection - courtesy of N.E.Preedy)

32) Late Spring sunshine greets the passing of another Leicester (Midland) engine, this time in the shape of LMS Class 4F 'Duck Six' 0-6-0 No 44182, as it plods along with a lengthy pick-up freight at Desborough and Rothwell, on 22nd April 1963. This station, situated between Kettering and Market Harborough was axed in 1968, four years after No 44182 had demised. (T.R.Amos)

33) The peace and quiet of South Wigston station, on the former Midland line from Rugby to Leicester, is disturbed by the presence of LMS Stanier 'Consul' Class 8F 2-8-0 No 48195, as it rattles a long rake of empty coal wagons along in April 1961, en-route for Market Harborough. No 48195, an 18A Toton inmate, moved on to fresh pastures at 18B Westhouses in June 1962, the same year as the closure of South Wigston station. (H.H.Bleads)

34) We pause in our travels at Leicester (Midland) station an important junction with a major passenger and freight engine shed. On 26th March 1966 steam working was all but at an end in the area. Photographed inside Leicester (London Road) station is a 'bulled up' LMS Class 8F 2-8-0 No 48467, from far off 8A Edge Hill (Liverpool) - with 15A Leicester (Midland) stencilled temporarily on the smokebox - with the RCTS 'Eight Counties' railtour to Nottingham. (F.Hornby)

35) What a difference a space of eight years makes in terms of both time and choice of locomotives. In the carriage sidings at Leicester in 1958 we find LMS Class 2P 4-4-0 No 40543, a firm favourite of Leicester (Midland) shed, at the head of a rake of carriages and sporting express headlamps. Looking at the building in the background, today one could hardly associate W.H.Smith & Son as 'Boot and Shoe Manufacturers'. (A.C.Ingram)

36) Moving from London Road station to the Midland shed, the yard of which could be seen from the former, we espy LMS *Jubilee* Class 4-6-0 No 45643 *Rodney,* a visitor from 2B Nuneaton in September 1963. From January 1960 to November 1961 (though not all at the same time) Leicester (Midland) had six *Jubilees* on its books, Nos 45585 *Hyderabad,* 45615 *Malay States,* 45616 *Malta G.C.,* 45636 *Uganda,* 45650 *Blake* and 45652 *Hawke.* (G.W.Sharpe)

37) In the latter years of its life Leicester (Midland) shed had a large covered roundhouse and turntable within, with a fairly large, but cramped yard with an exposed turntable and a modern concrete coaling plant. In steam in the yard in September 1963 is 17B Burton based LMS Class 8F 2-8-0 No 48694 which was destined to move to 16E Kirkby in March 1965 from Burton, a final home before withdrawal in March 1966. (G.W.Sharpe)

38) A final view of Leicester (Midland) shed before we continue our travels. On 15th June 1958, BR Class 2 2-6-0 No 78021, from 15B Kettering, takes a rest beside an unidentified LMS Class 3F 0-6-0 Tank, near to the ash disposal and coaling plants. The shed succumbed to the inevitable, closing its doors to steam on 13th June 1966, its last allocated engines being LMS Class 8F 2-8-0's and BR Class 2 2-6-0's. (W.G.Boyden)

39) At Syston Junction lines divide, one going off to Derby via Loughborough and Trent and another through Melton Mowbray to Nottingham. The Kettering to Nottingham route will be covered following a photo stop at Derby. 68A Carlisle (Kingmoor) based LMS Class 5 4-6-0 No 45083, fitted with a small snowplough, is a long way from home coupled to a guards van at Syston North Junction early in 1958. (A.C.Ingram)

40) Extremely flat countryside to the south of Sileby is the next venue, where LMS Class 8F 2-8-0 No 48395, from 16B Kirkby, toils past the camera with a seemingly never ending rake of down Class J mineral empties on 4th June 1962. Allocated to Kirkby from 18A Toton, in May 1958, No 48395 was destined to remain faithful to the former depot until it closed at the end of 1966, when it moved on to 8A Edge Hill (Liverpool). (B.W.L.Brooksbank)

41) Hathern, an intermediate station between Loughborough and Kegworth, proved a popular spot with this particular photographer as these next four pictures bear testament to, possibly because there were no station staff, apart from the signalman, to pester him, as it had been closed since 1960. LMS Class 8F 2-8-0 No 48350 (16A Toton) passes through with a northbound iron-ore train on 11th April 1964. (K.L.Seal)

42) A few days earlier, on 6th April 1964, LMS Class 8F 2-8-0 No 48221, another Toton locomotive, steams through Hathern station beneath a road bridge and heads for Trent with a down Class 7 mineral train. Both No 48221 and 48350 (above) were transferred away from Toton to 15C Kettering in June 1964. No 48221 eventually ended up at 8F Springs Branch Wigan, being condemned from there in February 1967. (K.L.Seal)

43) Relegated to a far more menial duty than it was originally designed for, LMS *Jubilee* Class 4-6-0 No 45556 *Nova Scotia* passes the derelict station and overgrown goods yard with a southbound Class 8 goods train on 11th April 1964. *Nova Scotia* is far off the normal beaten track being based at 5A Crewe (North) on the West Coast Main Line, being taken out of service from there five months later. (K.L.Seal)

44) A final action shot in this photo-feature of Hathern, is taken from the same vantage-point as the previous one and also taken on the same day. Steam and smoke from the safety valves and chimney of BR Class 9F 2-10-0 No 92070, from 15A Leicester (Midland) obscures the station as it heads through with another Class 8 loose-fitted freight heading southbound towards Loughborough. (K.L.Seal)

45) Smoke swirls from beneath the girder bridge flyover at Trent Junction from the exhaust of BR *Britannia* Class 4-6-2 No 70052 *Firth of Tay* as it heads towards Nottingham (Midland) with the continuation of the 'Notts. & Lincs. Railtour' (LCGB) from London (St.Pancras) - see Plate No 1 - on 24th April 1965. Until October 1962 *Firth of Tay* was based in Glasgow at 66A Polmadie and 67A Corkerhill before moving to 5A Crewe (North). (K.L.Seal)

46) A murky, fog-laden scene at Beeston, on the Midland Main Line to Nottingham, on 16th April 1963. Former Midland Railway Class 4F 0-6-0 No 43988, a 15C Leicester (Midland) inhabitant, passes a fine array of signals, most of which are at danger, with a lengthy freight train heading south from Nottingham. No 43988, of a Fowler design from 1911, soldiered on in revenue earning service until October 1964, being withdrawn from 15E Coalville. (K.L.Seal)

47) We pause for a while at the great former Midland Railway centre at Derby, birthplace of many a fine steam locomotive in years gone by, with a look at the station, shed and works. With the station in the background LMS Class 8F 2-8-0 No 48630, a rival to the Midland from 5B Crewe (South), cautiously negotiates point work as it moves away from the station light engine in 1962. (N.E.Preedy)

48) 17A Derby based LMS Class 2 2-6-2T No 46502 on a through road at Derby Station on 12th April 1959 is probably acting on station pilot duties. In the left background is the mighty workshops. To the right is the lengthy footbridge leading to the shed and works (a severe test for the temptations of spotters to 'bunk' the same, much to the wrath of foremen and shed-masters alike). (N.L.Browne)

49) A congested scene at Derby - circa 1956 - during the rebuilding of the station. On the left is a pick-up freight, complete with an immaculate guards van. In the centre 55D Royston allocated Class 8F 2-8-0 No 48070 threads through the wagons and coaching stock with a northbound freight train. Note the small snowplough affixed to the engine. No 48070 remained loyal to Royston until withdrawn from traffic in November 1967. (R.S.Carpenter)

50) With its driving wheels seven feet in diameter the beat of this LMS Class 2P 4-4-0 No 40364 is very measured as it pulls away from Derby on 25th August 1952, bound for its home shed at 17B Burton with a local passenger train. We can actually see a gap in the exhaust between one puff and another as is blackens the skyline. In later years, with mass withdrawals, many sidings near Derby station were packed with dead locos. (Peter Hay)

51) A duet of locomotives are photographed from the footbridge at Derby station in 1961, where we can also see a smattering of spotters on the platform. From left to right are: LMS *Jubilee* Class 4-6-0 No 45685 *Barfleur,* from 82E Bristol Barrow Road, and LMS Ivatt Class 2-6-0 No 46500, a local product from 17A. *Barfleur* demised from Barrow Road in April 1964, whereas No 46500 survived until January 1967, when it was condemned from 8L Aintree. (G.W.Sharpe)

52) One of the last surviving LMS Unrebuilt *Patriot* Class 4-6-0's No 45543 *Home Guard,* from 24L Carnforth, has a rest from its labours in the shed yard at 17A Derby, whilst being employed on the LCGB 'The Midland Limited Railtour' on 14th October 1962. Despite being in fine external condition this must have been one of the last workings for *Home Guard* as it was taken out of service the following month. (N.E.Preedy)

53) An elevated 'watchtower' overlooks the yard at Derby on 7th June 1953 where a lined out LMS Class 4P 'Compound' 4-4-0 No 41195 rests out of steam. Allocated to 22B Gloucester (Barnwood) at this stage in time, records show it was still based there in November 1957 when it was rendered surplus to requirements. Derby Works disposed of the remains during the same month. (A.N.H.Glover)

54) Many types of steam engines visited Derby shed for one reason or another. Standing in the open next to the exposed roundhouse on 9th September 1962, in apparently ex. works condition, is former Crosti-boilered BR Class 9F 2-10-0 No 92029, from 15B Kettering. In the far left distance is an unidentified BR Class 5 4-6-0. 9th September 1962 was a significant milestone in time - the beginning of the mass slaughter of steam. (T.R.Amos)

55) Two locomotives from the Eastern Region are fresh from overhaul awaiting a final painting job at 17A Derby on 1st November 1959. In the foreground is LMS Class 8F 2-8-0 No 48331, based at 41E Staveley (Barrow Hill) behind which is LMS Class 4F 0-6-0 No 44521, from 31F Peterborough (Spital Bridge). Derby shed, recoded 16C in September 1963, finally closed its doors to steam on 6th March 1967. (A.N.H.Glover)

56) Derby Works hosts BR *Britannia* Class 4-6-2 No 70012 *John of Gaunt,* a 5B Crewe (South) locomotive, during an open day on 28th August 1965. Apart from being at Crewe (South), this 1951 built Pacific, seen here devoid of nameplates, had spells at 32A Norwich, 32D Yarmouth South Town, 30A Stratford, 31B March, 1A Willesden, 5A Crewe (North), 6G Llandudno Junction and 12A Carlisle (Kingmoor) in its sixteen year life. (K.L.Seal)

57) On what appears to be another open day, in August 1964, 16C Derby based LMS Class 5 4-6-0 No 44888 stands between Derby shed and the works as enthusiasts scuttle about, notebooks in hand. In comparison with most railway depots the larger workshops were almost impossible to get round without an official pass as many a spotter found to his cost - sometimes financially - Derby Works was no exception. (D.K.Jones)

58) The interior of the steam repair shop at Derby is all but empty on 13th January 1963. BR Class 4 4-6-0 No 75045, from 27A Bank Hall, Liverpool, occupies one bay whilst its tender is in another. 1963 was the last year for steam overhauls at Derby Works, which ceased on 20th September with the return of BR Class 4 4-6-0 No 75042, a Derby allocated example - rather apt for the occasion. This left only Crewe and Horwich on the LMR. (D.K.Jones)

59) We retrace our steps and head south for a four page spread taken between Kettering and Melton Mowbray on the former Midland line which avoided Leicester. Ex. Midland Railway Class 4F 0-6-0 No 43861, a resident of 15A Wellingborough, coasts along between Harringworth and Gretton with a Nottingham (Midland) to Kettering local passenger train in 1958. (A.C.Ingram)

60) One of the more 'unsung' members of the LMS *Royal Scot* Class 4-6-0's No 46103 *Royal Scots Fusilier,* based at 14B Kentish Town, canters through the closed Harringworth station with a Bradford to St.Pancras express in the Summer of 1959. Observe the two different sizes of signal posts in the foreground. After spells at Saltley and Carlisle (Upperby) in 1961/62, No 46103 ended its days at 55A Leeds (Holbeck). (A.C.Ingram)

61) Taken at the same spot, but in the previous year, LMS Class 8F 2-8-0 No 48645, from 15B Kettering, storms through Harringworth with an up mineral train bound for Corby steelworks. Both the locomotive and Corby steelworks are long gone. No 48645 was transferred to 18A Toton in February 1962, but returned to Kettering the following month. It later served from Leicester (Midland), Colwick, Saltley and Chester sheds. (A.C.Ingram)

62) LMS Hughes Class 6P5F 'Crab' Class 2-6-0 No 42759, a 14A Cricklewood engine, rounds a curve on the approaches to Harringworth station, closed in 1948, at the head of a down express freight consisting of closed wagons in 1958. Unlike many other classes the 'Crabs' tended to stay at depots for quite long periods of time. Between January 1959 and withdrawal in January 1963, No 42759 only had two homes - at 17B Burton and 9G Gorton. (A.C.Ingram)

63) LMS Stanier *Jubilee* Class 4-6-0 No 45618 *New Hebrides,* one of the stud of 14B Kentish Town engines, bursts out of Seaton Tunnel and heads northbound in a flurry of smoke and steam whilst in charge of a relief express from St.Pancras in August 1958. *New Hebrides* was one of a large number of *Jubilee's* which ended its working life based at Burton shed, being condemned in March 1964 and disposed of by Looms of Spondon. (A.C.Ingram)

64) The upgrade is not assisting former Midland Railway Class 3F 0-6-0 No 43499, from 15B Kettering, which is laying a smoke-screen as she approaches Seaton Tunnel with the return 'Manton pick-up' from Oakham to Kettering in 1960. Once the diesels began to flood the Midland Division elderly locomotives like this were rapidly swept away. In the case of No 43499 it was sent to 9G Gorton (Manchester) in June 1960. (A.C.Ingram)

65) 14B Kentish Town had quite a number of LMS Class 5 4-6-0s on its books until 1962. One of them, No 44812, is photographed from over the top of the northern end of Seaton Tunnel, as it is about to plunge into the depths with an up eight coach relief express bound for St.Pancras in 1958. In November of the following year No 44812 was drafted to 21A Saltley, where it had a spell of six and a half years before moving on again. (A.C.Ingram)

66) We take our leave of Harringworth and Seaton Tunnel with this parting shot of Crosti-boilered BR Class 9F 2-10-0 No 92027, a 15A Wellingborough engine, as it emerges from the north end of the tunnel with a down partially fitted goods in the late 1950's. Seaton Tunnel burrowed beneath the Market Harborough to Stamford line which included Seaton station, closed in 1966. (A.C.Ingram)

67) We do an about turn and move north once again, this time to Nottingham (Midland). Having no doubt been under shelter within the station after a downpour, a young lad and his companion venture on to the platform and head towards LMS *Jubilee* Class 4-6-0 No 45627 *Sierra Leone,* 16A Nottingham, which is in charge of a down express on 31st May 1959. No doubt that they were about to ask, "Can we cab you mate?" to the crew. (F.Hornby)

68) Transferred to 16A Nottingham from 15B Kettering in November 1959, BR Class 2 2-6-0 No 78021 finds itself on station pilot duty on 17th July 1961, light engine between duties. No 78021 remained loyal to Nottingham shed for just over four years before moving not too far away to 16C Derby. In the left background is a variety of railway bric-a-brac and also several bricked-up arches beneath the road bridge. (D.K.Jones)

69) Steam and smoke are highlighted by bright sunshine which envelopes Nottingham (Midland) station on 24th April 1965. LMS Class 4F 0-6-0 No 44401, from 16E Kirkby, minus shedplate has 16E stencilled in its place, as it combines with 40B Immingham allocated LNER B1 Class 4-6-0 No 61406 for a Locomotive Club of Great Britain special. Despite being thrust into the public limelight No 44401 was condemned two months later. (N.E.Preedy)

70) It was not uncommon for LNER locomotives to visit Nottingham (Midland), mostly in the shape of Thompson B1 Class 4-6-0's, but in the days before the diesel multiple units, other, more elderly types were to be seen there. Former Great Eastern Railway D16/3 Class 4-4-0 No 62571, based at 40A Lincoln, puts in an appearance in 1957 on a Lincoln to Derby local passenger. By the end of the following year it was on the scrap-heap. (M.F.Higson)

71) A youngster gazes in awe from a platform at Nottingham (Midland) at BR Class 2 2-6-0 No 78028, a local engine from 16A, as it stands in the station with a train of tank wagons in May 1961. Young as he is, the seeds are already being sown for a long and fruitful trainspotting career. In the left of the picture is Riddles WD Class 8F 2-8-0 No 90504, from 2F Woodford Halse. (C.Hughes)

72) A wet and gloomy day fits the bill for the end of the operational road for the famous LMS *Royal Scot* Class 4-6-0 No 46100 *Royal Scot* on 18th November 1962. Seen here with a partially sacked chimney in the store line at 16A Nottingham a few weeks after official withdrawal. Having pounded up and down the WCML for many a year No 46100 was transferred to the Midland Division in November 1959. It is now preserved at Bressingham. (J.Schatz)

73) Locally based BR Class 5 4-6-0 No 73017 sports express headlamps whilst being coupled to a wagon in the yard at 16A Nottingham - circa 1956, a few years after construction. The 172 members of this class were constructed between 1951 and 1957 and were very successful in their capacity as mixed traffic engines. Despite the mass influx of diesel power in the sixties the first examples of the class were not withdrawn until 1964. (N.E.Preedy)

74) The large and spacious shed at Nottingham had three sheltered roundhouses which once accommodated a large fleet of steam locomotives, both ancient and modern. One of its elder examples, LMS Class 2P 4-4-0 No 40454, looking in fine external condition, is in the company of LMS Class 4F 0-6-0 No 44577, another resident, inside one of the roundhouses in March 1955. The shed closed to steam around April 1965. (D.K.Jones)

75) We cannot leave the Nottingham area without a fleeting visit to the huge depot at 18A Toton, a freight complex on the west side of the main running lines between Long Eaton, Sandiacre and Stapleford stations. This shed had a huge allocation of engines mostly consisting of LMS Class 4F 0-6-0's, LMS Class 8F 2-8-0's and BR Class 9F 2-10-0's, including No 92081 photographed in the yard on 30th September 1956. (A.N.H.Glover)

76) A line-up of Midland Railway and LMS Class 4F 0-6-0's in the shed yard at Toton on 7th April 1963. They include, from left to right, Nos 44200, 44213 and 43947. The writing was on the wall at this date in time for these particular engines at Toton. No 43947 departed in October 1963 (9L Buxton), 44200 to 8G Sutton Oak the same month and 44213 to 16E Kirkby in November 1963. (K.L.Seal)

77) Former Midland Railway Class OF 0-4-0ST No 41518 takes a rest in Toton shed yard as a visitor from 18D Staveley (Barrow Hill) on 12th August 1956, dwarfed by an unidentified LMS Class 8F 2-8-0. When it was withdrawn in February 1958 it was the last surviving example from the original class of ten units. Eight of their number were taken out of service between 1922 and 1932 leaving the two survivors as oddities on the railway scene. (J.D.Gomersall)

78) A panoramic view of the shed yard at Toton on 7th April 1963 shows two of its stud of LMS Class 3F 'Jinty' 0-6-0 Tanks out of steam in the foreground, Nos 47223 and 47645. The former had only been at Toton for a month (transferred from 14A Cricklewood). The latter had come from the same depot in September of the previous year. In the background is No 47466, withdrawn from 18B Westhouses in September 1962. (K.L.Seal)

79) In another section of the yard on the same day is BR Class 9F 2-10-0 No 92156, allocated to Toton from new in November 1957. To the left of No 92156 is a sister engine, hemmed between a shack and a wagon. To the right of No 92156 are a motley duo of carriages. Toton changed codes from 18A to 16A in September 1963 and officially closed to steam in late 1965, but it did not sever its links until November 1966. (K.L.Seal)

80) A begrimed LMS Beyer-Garratt nears the end of its working life on 6th June 1956. 2-6-6-2T No 47981, working in reverse, trails a lengthy freight train along near to the marshalling yards at Toton. Thirty-three of these engines were constructed for use on the LMS, the last survivors working from 18C Hasland. All were withdrawn between June 1955 and April 1958, No 47981 being condemned in November 1956. (N.L.Browne)

81) Tracking northwards from Nottingham our next port of call is at Alfreton and South Normanton station. With upper semaphores raised in all directions former Midland Railway Class 4F 0-6-0 No 43850, from 18B Westhouses, wheels an up mineral (Class J) freight along on 23rd June 1961. This station closed in 1967 being replaced by a more spartan structure (Alfreton and Mansfield Parkway) which today has only two tracks. (B.W.L.Brooksbank)

82) Our next stop is at Chesterfield for a two page feature of predominately former Midland Railway power. Signals are at danger in the distance to guard the exit of Class 3F 0-6-0 No 43211, of 18C Hasland, as it eases a pick-up goods out of sidings on 5th September 1957 as the loco crew enjoy the late summer sunshine. No 43211 was originally designed for the Somerset & Dorset Joint Railway, but is a long way from home. (Peter Hay)

83) MR Class 3F 0-6-0 No 43321, based at 55E Normanton on the North Eastern Region, takes the avoiding line at Chester-field with a loose-fitted freight on the same date as the above picture. A lone railwayman in the left of the frame looks towards the camera, as do three others to the right of the goods. The vintage of the carriage on the left in use as a shelter for railway workers is unknown. (Peter Hay)

84) After a good night's rest the photographer returned to Chesterfield the following day to record two further pictures for posterity. LMS Class 4P 'Compound' 4-4-0 No 41156 (21B Bournville) and LMS *Jubilee* Class 4-6-0 No 45569 *Tasmania*, from 55A Leeds Holbeck, blast their way northwards through Chesterfield station with the down *Thames-Clyde Express* from St.Pancras to St.Enoch. (Peter Hay)

85) Midland Railway Class 3F 0-6-0 No 43321 is still on duty from the previous day and prepares to depart from the scene piloting MR Class 4F 0-6-0 No 43987, from 55B Stourton, with a loose-coupled freight, presumably bound for a destination on the North Eastern Region. By 1963 both locomotives had gone from active service, No 43321 in February 1961 (55E) and No 43987 in July 1963 (55B). (Peter Hay)

86) Almost mid-way between Chesterfield and Sheffield is Dore, known as the Dore and Totley triangle in railway terms with a line going off to Edale and Chinley in the Peak District. With the driver looking upwards to the photographer BR Class 5 4-6-0 No 73171, from 55A Leeds (Holbeck), heads southbound on the main line with a parcels train after passing through Dore station in the summer of 1958. No 73171 was the last member of the class to be constructed. (G.W.Sharpe)

87) The approach to Dore station, from this angle, is on the upgrade, as can be seen by the catch point in the foreground. It is also in an extremely pleasant setting with lush greenery surrounding it. LMS Class 6P5F 'Crab' 2-6-0 No 42827, from 21A Saltley, disturbs the rustic tranquility as it steams in with a passenger train in August 1960. (H.H.Bleads)

88) Millhouses shed was the depot which provided Midland line power out of Sheffield (Midland), coded 19B. In February 1958 it was taken over by the Eastern Region, changing codes to 41C which it retained until closure on 1st January 1962. Types once housed here included LMS *Jubilee* and *Royal Scot* Class 4-6-0's. LMS Class 4P 'Compound' 4-4-0 No 41089 is a visitor to the shed from 21B Bournville (Birmingham) on 7th April 1957. (N.L.Browne)

89) A cast-iron overbridge and water tower look down upon LMS *Jubilee* Class 4-6-0 No 45639 *Raleigh* as it steams and sizzles in readiness for the off from Sheffield (Midland) station with an express in 1960. *Raleigh,* a 55A Leeds (Holbeck) engine was a regular performer, like many sister locos, on passenger services through this station until the diesels took over. It was withdrawn from Holbeck shed in October 1963. (G.W.Sharpe)

90) As well as the *Jubilee's,* LMS *Royal Scot* Class 4-6-0's were also to be seen daily on expresses on the former Midland main lines - until ousted by diesels. On 13th July 1962 No 46158 The *Loyal Regiment,* in a very clean condition and obviously looked after by its owners at 9E Trafford Park, waits in a siding at Sheffield (Midland) to take over a passenger working in drizzly and misty conditions. (J.Schatz)

91) An all but deserted scene at Sheffield (Midland), in railway movement terms. A small group of railwaymen pass the time of day chatting on the platform on 13th July 1962. Occupying a bay platform is 16A Nottingham based BR Class 4 4-6-0 No 75064 at the head of a local passenger to Nottingham. Allocated to 16A from new in June 1957 it moved on to 17A Derby two months after this picture was taken. (J.Schatz)

92) An unsightly water column brazier appears to be guarding the tender of LMS Class 5 4-6-0 No 45073, a 9E Trafford Park engine, as it takes on fresh water supplies under the watchful gaze of several interested onlookers at Sheffield (Midland) on 3rd September 1966. No 45073 has just brought in the 9.45 am (Saturdays only) Manchester to Yarmouth express almost at the end of the summer service timetable. (M.S.Stokes)

93) A tall wooden posted upper semaphore shows a clear road ahead for LMS Class 4F 0-6-0 No 44446, in a filthy condition, as it wheezes along on the up slow line at Kilnhurst, between Leeds and Sheffield on the ex. Midland main line, with a coal train bound for Roundwood sidings in April 1965. Note the yellow stripe on the cab-side of this 55D Royston locomotive denoting prohibition south of Crewe on the WCML. (M.S.Stokes)

94) Another 55D Royston locomotive, in an even worse external condition than the one above, MR Class 4F 0-6-0 No 43983, is at the same location in February 1965 and is struggling for adhesion with a rake of loaded mineral wagons. Despite its unkempt appearance No 43983 managed to struggle on at Royston for a further six months. Scrapping took place far from home at Cashmores, Newport at the end of 1965. (M.S.Stokes)

95) A splendid panoramic view of the approaches to Normanton station in the late 1950's. There are signals of all shapes and sizes and sidings galore as far as the eye can see. In the right of the picture is the former Lancashire and Yorkshire shed which continued to house and service steam until closure in the Autumn of 1967. In the centre LMS *Jubilee* Class 4-6-0 No 45575 *Madras* (14B Kentish Town) heads the *Thames-Clyde Express.* (Stuart Pitchforth)

96) Steam Railways have always been associated with smoke and grime especially in an industrial or inner city setting. This picture bears testimony to the same as can be seen by the smoke-tainted buildings in the left of this picture in the City of Leeds. LMS Class 8F 2-8-0 No 48473 (55D Royston) is the epitome of filth as it passes Wortley Junction with a northbound freight in August 1966. (M.S.Stokes)

97) Multi-trackwork at Leeds fills the frame of this photograph with an array of signals in the background in this June 1960 recording of *The Waverley* express at speed with LMS Class 5 4-6-0 No 45384, from far away 67A Corkerhill (Glasgow), leading LMS *Royal Scot* Class 4-6-0 No 46145 *The Duke of Wellington's Regt. (West Riding),* allocated to 55A Leeds (Holbeck). (G.W.Sharpe)

98) Two different coloured lamps on the bufferbeam indicate that this is an express though its progress has been hampered by a signal restriction on 21st February 1961. The driver of 55A Leeds (Holbeck) based LMS *Jubilee* Class 4-6-0 No 45605 *Cyprus* peers from the cab of his charge at an unknown location within Leeds. The obelisk style building to the right might be a 'folly' - of no practical use of any kind. (D.J.Jones)

99) The dark interior of Leeds City station is filled with smoke and steam from a number of locomotives within, as BR Class 4 2-6-4T No 80118 (50B Leeds - Neville Hill) pilots LNER A3 Class 4-6-2 No 60086 *Gainsborough,* also from Neville Hill, as they depart with an express - circa 1958. Like the other members of the Class *Gainsborough* gained a double chimney (June 1959), but not German smoke deflectors. (D.K.Jones)

100) A contrast of colour light and semaphore signals at Leeds City station in May 1957. Bearing the old 'Lion & Wheel' logo on its tender, 55A Leeds (Holbeck) LMS *Jubilee* Class 4-6-0 No 45565 *Victoria* waits with an express. Perhaps the train is running late for the driver is looking at what appears to be a 'fed-up' fire man leaning against a gas lamp. Holbeck liked its *Jubilee's* and kept them consistently for many years. (G.W.Sharpe)

101) Bright sunlight filters through the cavernous ornate roof and highlights the steam drifting upwards from the safety valves of LMS *Jubilee* Class 4-6-0 No 45600 *Bermuda,* a visitor to Leeds City station from 26F Patricroft. *Bermuda* is departing with the 12.35 pm to Manchester (Exchange) on Saturday 18th August 1962. A longstanding Patricroft engine, *Bermuda* was reluctantly transferred to 9D Newton Heath in January 1965. (J.D.Gomersall)

102) A large hoarding advertising the services of John Whitehead & Son Ltd - printers, lithographers and bookbinders - occupies a prime position overlooking the east end of Leeds City station — circa 1955. LNER *Shire* D49 Class 4-4-0 No 62751 *The Albrighton,* from 50E Scarborough, is the main subject matter of this print. It remained at Scarborough until being taken out of traffic in March 1959. (D.K.Jones)

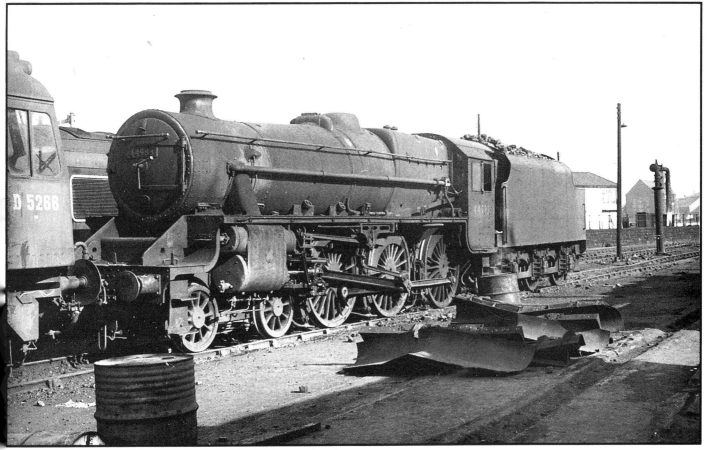

103) We turn our attention to the depot which has supplied us with a number of locomotives seen in print in this album - 55A Leeds (Holbeck). Despite the presence of diesels on 19th September 1965 Holbeck still maintained quite a large stud of steam engines, including one of its LMS Class 5 4-6-0's No 44983, seen resting in the yard between duties. Yet another longstanding inmate it survived until closure to steam in 1967. (R.Hennefer)

104) The two large roundhouses at Holbeck still housed a number of locomotives on 14th August 1967, though most of the large passenger types had long departed, either being transferred elsewhere or sent for scrap. On view in this photograph, from left to right are: LMS Class 4 2-6-4T No 42283 (56F Low Moor), LMS Class 5 4-6-0's Nos 44983 and 44826 (both 55A engines) and LMS Class 4 2-6-0 No 43084, also of Holbeck. (Ken Ellis)

105) Having replenished its tender with coal, a more than generous quota, LMS *Royal Scot* Class 4-6-0 No 46108 *Seaforth Highlander,* from 12B Carlisle (Upperby), has retired to a back road at Holbeck shed to await its next turn of duty on a misty day in 1962. In the late fifties *Seaforth Highlander* had been based at 55A. It also had spells at Longsight (Manchester), Preston and Crewe (North) before going to Upperby, its last home. (B.J.Miller)

106) Turning our attention to the Bradford area briefly we catch a glimpse of LMS Class 4 2-6-4 Tanks Nos 42073 and 42094, both from 56C Copley Hill, as they double-head a Bradford (Exchange) to Kings Cross express at Mill Lane Junction, Bradford on 5th August 1961. Both locos will come off the train at Leeds (Central) to be replaced by a larger engine with extra carriages added on. Today, No 42073 is preserved at Lakeside. (D.K.Jones)

107) Kirkstall, between Leeds and Shipley, with its four tracks is the setting for LMS *Jubilee* Class 4-6-0 No 45697 *Achilles,* yet another 55A Leeds (Holbeck) engine, as it speeds towards the camera with an eight coach St.Pancras to St.Enoch express on 20th August 1966. For many years a Carlisle (Kingmoor) loco *Achilles* found its way to Holbeck in February 1964 via Blackpool and Bank Hall. Withdrawal came in September 1967. (M.S.Stokes)

108) For operating reasons the North Eastern Region adopted a policy of employing tank engines on expresses to and from Leeds to Bradford. LMS Class 4 2-6-4T No 42394 (55A Leeds - Holbeck), without the luxury of a side-window cab, drifts into the spacious station at Calverley & Rodley with the 12.15 pm St.Pancras to Bradford express on 26th June 1964. Note the tall signal post elevated above the station building. (B.W.L.Brooksbank)

109) A large factory complex on the right looks down upon Calverley & Rodley station on the same date as the above picture. A less than well kept LMS Class 5 4-6-0 No 45092, a 10A Carnforth loco, rounds a curve with up empties. Calverley & Rodley is showing signs of neglect in the upper photo as the overgrown weeds next to No 42394 testify to. It is therefore not surprising it closed during 1965 echoing the fate of many others. (B.W.L.Brooksbank)

110) Sporting the customary express headlamps LMS Class 4 2-6-4T No 42093, an inhabitant of 55F Bradford (Manningham), looks the worse for wear as it passes a cluster of signal gantries at Shipley. No 42093 is in charge of a Birmingham (New Street) to Bradford train on 16th March 1967, shortly before being reallocated to 55E Normanton, its last depot from where it was condemned in October 1967. After a period of storage No 42093 was cut up at Drapers, Hull. (N.E.Preedy)

111) A 'Crow's Nest' view of Shipley station as seen from a lofty vantage-point - circa 1956. Coal supplies appear to be at a minimum in the bunker of LMS Class 4 2-6-4T No 42052, a 55F Bradford (Manningham) inmate, as it steams in with a local passenger train. This was the second station to be built replacing an earlier structure originally constructed in the nineteenth century - situated on the Bradford line. (R.Butterfield)

112) Returning to the main Leeds to Carlisle line we find ourselves at Saltaire, a few short miles from Shipley. BR Class 5 4-6-0 No 73012 blasts through the station with a St.Pancras to Edinburgh express in the early fifties. Later in the decade No 73012 was drafted to the Western Region at 82C Swindon, serving later from Llanelly and Bristol Barrow Road sheds. Saltaire station disappeared from the public eye during 1965. (R.Butterfield)

113) The famous mill town of Keighley is featured next. LMS *Royal Scot* Class 4-6-0 No 46113 *Cameronian,* from 55A Leeds (Holbeck), approaches with the *Thames-Clyde Express* on 20th December 1958. Despite having smoke deflectors, dark, black smoke enshrouds the boiler and cab, partially obscuring the driver's view. Today, Keighley is the junction for the preserved Keighley and Worth Valley Railway, which is always worth a visit. (D.K.Jones)

114) Moving out into the sticks, amidst pleasant rolling countryside, we espy LMS *Jubilee* Class 4-6-0 No 45573 *Newfoundland,* again at the head of the *Thames-Clyde Express,* near to Cononley, the nearest intermediate station to Skipton, on 29th June 1960. *Newfoundland* was a firm favourite at 55A Leeds (Holbeck) remaining there until condemned in September 1965 the same year that Cononley station was closed for good. (D.K.Jones)

115) Skipton was once an important junction for lines leading to Colne, Burnley, Grassington and Ilkley, as well as being on the main Leeds to Carlisle line. The structure seen in this photograph on 13th June 1964 was the second to be built. This is a fine view of both the station and town - looking south. An unidentified LMS Class 5 is in charge of a down semi-fast and a diesel multiple unit occupies another platform. (F.Hornby)

116) Brilliant summer sunshine encompasses the station and surroundings at Skipton on 6th August 1960. Steam leaks from various points on a far from home LMS Class 5 4-6-0 No 45088 - 21A Saltley, in Birmingham - in charge of a local passenger working. Abandoned by Saltley in August 1963 No 45088 found a new home at 15C Leicester (Midland). A final move three months later took it to 16C Derby. (Derek Singleton)

(17) Skipton was important enough to have its own Motive Power Depot built by the Midland Railway and first coded 20F by British Railways in 1948. Between 1950 and 1963 there were a number of shedcode changes - 23A, back to 20F, 24G and finally 10G. Early in 1967 LMS *Jubilee* Class 4-6-0 No 45593 *Kolhapur* (since preserved) puts in an appearance at the shed. Note the yellow stripe on the cab and the 'bulled-up' buffers. (G.W.Sharpe)

(18) The allocation at Skipton shed was never very large at any one time, consisting mainly of elderly 0-6-0's and Tank engine types. One of the latter, in the shape of LMS Class 3F 0-6-0T No 47427, a longstanding Skipton inmate, takes a rest between shunting duties in the west yard on 28th September 1963. The shed closed on 3rd April 1967 its last allocation of engines being BR Class 4 4-6-0's. (H.L.Holland)

119) Moving along the main line for a few miles we pause for a while at Hellifield where a line to Blackburn once went. Locally based LMS Class 4F 0-6-0 No 44149 passes its home and enters Hellifield station with a goods train on 6th August 1960. The number '83' on the bufferbeam is somewhat of a mystery. Having been a Hellifield engine for many years No 44149 did not part company with the same until July 1963 - going to Skipton. (Derek Singleton)

120) A view of part of the station, shed and shed yard on 24th September 1960 which includes the antiquated wooden coaling stage facility. Nearest the camera is a usurper from the LNER, Thompson B1 Class 4-6-0 No 61069, a 50A York locomotive. In the left background is Hellifield based MR Class 3F 0-6-0 No 43756. Despite its early vintage No 43756 was destined to remain in traffic at Hellifield until condemned in September 1962. (Derek Singleton)

121) A regiment of steam enthusiasts carrying cameras jostle for prime positions beside the track at Hellifield on 15th February 1965 in order to gain the best shots of LMS *Royal Scot* Class 4-6-0 No 46115 *Scots Guardsman*. No 46115 is in charge of the Railway Correspondence & Travel Society 'Royal Scot Commemorative Railtour'. The train will shortly depart for Carlisle via the Settle & Carlisle line. (H.L.Holland)

122) As part of a tour of Scottish sheds in May 1950 Hellifield shed was also on the venue. A gaggle of spotters mill round in the background. In the foreground is former Midland Railway Class 1P 0-4-4T No 58033, a local engine, with a pair of drivers missing. Like Skipton, Hellifield had a number of different shedcodes under BR ownership - 20G (twice), 23B and 24H. It closed to operational steam on 17th June 1963. (A.J.Pike)

123) Travelling towards Carlisle from Hellifield the next station on the Settle & Carlisle is at Long Preston. An upper quadrant signal is raised to allow for the passage of 8F Springs Branch Wigan LMS Class 5 4-6-0 No 45449 into the station, which is about to rattle its local passenger train, from Hellifield to Carlisle, over the sleepered crossing point on 10th May 1963. (J.M.Tolson)

124) Despite it being Spring there is sparse foliage on the trees in the background. A solitary female passenger and a member of the station staff at Long Preston shelter under the canopy of the small waiting room as LMS Class 5 4-6-0 No 44758, from 24J Lancaster (Green Ayre), glides into the platform with a Leeds City to Carnforth and Morecambe local stopping train. (J.M.Tolson)

125) High Summer on 20th July 1961 and the trees in the previous picture are in full bloom, enjoying the warm sunshine. Photographed from an overbridge LMS *Jubilee* Class 4-6-0 No 45562 *Alberta,* possibly 55A Leeds (Holbeck's) favourite member of the class, roars towards the camera at the head of a St.Pancras to Glasgow (St.Enoch) express. This view shows the delights of this tidy rural station with its well kept 'gardens'. (D.K.Jones)

126) The line to Clapham and Carnforth leaves us at Settle Junction and staying on the main line at Settle station we find a splendid nameboard by the platform. For those of you with less than good eyesight the board reads 'SETTLE' - altitude 510 feet - population 2300 - with the badges of 'SETTLE & WEST RIDING OF YORKSHIRE'. On the arrows some of the lettering reads 'Settle', 'Settle Down', 'Settle Up' & 'Enter'. (J.M.Tolson)

127) On the 10th May 1963 the photographer had the foresight to capture on film both the embellished nameboard at Settle and also here at Horton-in-Ribblesdale where the population compared to Settle has dropped considerably. It would be interesting to compare the population of both towns today compared with 1963! The sign also shows us that London is 242 miles away and that we are at an altitude of 850 feet. (J.M.Tolson)

128) There is an air of neglect in this picture of Horton-in- Ribblesdale on a murky day in 1965. This may well be a Sunday for LMS Class 5 4-6-0 No 45254, allocated at 12A Carlisle (Kingmoor), is working 'wrong line' into the stone built station with special express (1X 57). Horton-in-Ribblesdale closed 'officially' for the use of normal passenger trains in 1970. Thankfully the line itself has now been saved. (D.K.Jones)

129) Possibly because of its remoteness not too many pictures of many parts of the old Settle & Carlisle route appear to be available. The next four prints are devoted to various locations on the line, some unknown. Clouds hang low over the moorland hills in the background and clumps of hardy grass brave the spartan conditions on 22nd September 1967, as LMS Class 5 4-6-0 No 45078 (8F Springs Branch Wigan) heads a freight train. (W.Piggott)

130) A stone built house in the background is almost lost in the grim and rugged countryside at Ais Gill station in March 1967. Smoke-blackened BR Class 5 'Caprotti' 4-6-0 No 73157, from 9H Patricroft in Manchester, labours up the incline with a heavy relief express (1N 62). With its shedplate long gone the shedcode of 9H has been crudely stencilled on the smokebox door in large white letters. (D.K.Jones)

131) During 1967 the line from Leeds to Carlisle was used and followed by more enthusiasts than in any other previous year. This was due in the main, especially during the Summer service, to the surviving 55A Leeds (Holbeck) LMS *Jubilee*'s being employed on express duties. On an unspecified day in September 1967 the focus of attention is on No 45593 *Kolhapur* with a passenger train near to Ribblehead Viaduct. (Mike Turner)

132) This fine and evocative picture sums up the brooding majesty of the Settle & Carlisle line. The peak in the left background is obscured by low mist and cloud, a sign of worsening weather in the Winter months to come. In the aftermath of a squall, a rather less than clean 12A Carlisle (Kingmoor) BR Class 9F 2-10-0 No 92051, with a home-made numberplate, battles its way up to what is presumably Ais Gill summit in September 1967 with a lengthy goods. (Mike Turner)

133) We depart from the Settle & Carlisle line and arrive at Carlisle, a most important railway junction town in the days of steam where in times gone by locomotives from many different railway companies used to meet. On a wet day in 1958, 55A Leeds (Holbeck) *Royal Scot* Class 4-6-0 No 46112 *Sherwood Forester* takes the line towards Leeds with the up *Thames-Clyde Express.* (G.W.Sharpe)

134) During the fifties and sixties three steam depots served the needs of Carlisle and its visiting engines - Canal (North British), Kingmoor (Caledonian) and Upperby (London & North Western). Locos employed on the line to Leeds and St.Pancras were usually serviced at Kingmoor and Upperby. A Kingmoor based BR *Clan* Class 4-6-2 No 72007 *Clan Mackintosh* stands nameless and minus a pair of drivers at Upperby on 25th April 1965. (T.R.Amos)

135) The pioneer Stanier Pacific LMS *Princess* Class 4-6-2 No 46200 *The Princess Royal* is in a state of limbo with a sacked chimney at Carlisle (Upperby) on 20th October 1963, thirty years after having been constructed at Crewe Works and almost twelve months after being withdrawn from Kingmoor shed. After a two year period of storage *The Princess Royal* was finally disposed of at Connels, Coatbridge in October 1964. A sad end. (R.Hennefer)

136) LMS *Coronation* Class 4-6-2 No 46238 *City of Carlisle* basks in warm sunshine in the yard of its home shed at Upperby in May 1964, five months before the class was ousted for ever on the West Coast Main Line. Built at Crewe in 1939, *City of Carlisle* was originally in a streamlined condition. It died at Upperby in October 1964. Upperby shed closed its doors to steam on 12th December 1966, but was used for storage for some time after this date. (R.W.Hinton)

137) The external state of 12A Carlisle (Kingmoor) BR *Clan* Class 4-6-2 No 72008 *Clan Macleod* makes a mockery of the fact that it was only twelve years old when this picture was taken on 30th March 1964. *Clan Macleod* is being employed on an Easter Monday extra local passenger which is departing from Carlisle (Citadel) for the north. The end for *Clan Macleod* came in April 1966, after only fourteen years of active duty. (H.L.Holland)

138) Steam erupts beneath the smoke-blackened facia of the station roof at Carlisle (Citadel) from LMS *Jubilee* Class 4-6-0 No 45605 *Cyprus* and LMS *Royal Scot* Class 4-6-0 No 46109 *Royal Engineer,* both of 55A Leeds (Holbeck), as they combine to double-head the up *Thames-Clyde Express* on the leg to Leeds in October 1952. To the right of *Cyprus* is a station pilot in the shape of LMS Class 3F 0-6-0T No 47415 from Upperby shed. (R.Butterfield)

139) Locomotives of all shapes and sizes and from different regions were a common feature of everyday life at Carlisle (Citadel). A Scottish example puts in an appearance at the station on 8th April 1957. Former North British Railway D30 Class 4-4-0 No 62423 *Dugald Dalgetty* waits in a bay platform with a local passenger train bound for the Waverley route and its home at 64G Hawick. It was withdrawn at the end of 1957. (R.Butterfield)

140) By the mid-sixties visits by 'foreign' locomotives were becoming rarer by the day. Although in an unkempt condition LNER V2 Class 2-6-2 No 60885, from 51A Darlington, is greeted with joy as it backs onto special train No 1X 90 at Citadel station at 4.25 pm on 8th June 1965. This express had been diesel hauled from Euston with 'Peak' Class 1Co-Co 1 Type 4 No D115 (to Crewe) & EE Type 4 No D374 (Crewe to Carlisle). (Ken Ellis)

141) LMS *Royal Scot* Class 4-6-0 No 46130 *The West Yorkshire Regiment* (55A Leeds - Holbeck) lets off steam as it departs from Citadel station with the 10.35 am Leeds (City) to Glasgow (St.Enoch) express on 3rd September 1962. *The West Yorkshire Regiment* had only three months to live after this picture was taken, being condemned from Holbeck in December 1962. Crewe Works claimed the remains in October 1963. (J.M.Tolson)

142) The peaceful waters of the River Eden flow gently beneath Etterby Bridge, to the north of Carlisle on 17th June 1967. With the bulk of Carlisle acting as a backcloth LMS Class 5 4-6-0 No 45013 rattles a mixed fitted freight over the bridge and heads northbound. No 45013 was a longstanding occupant of Carlisle (Kingmoor) shed and it did not break its ties with the depot until it closed in January 1968. (N.E.Preedy)

143) LMS Fowler Class 4 2-6-4T No 42301 at rest in the yard of its base at 12A Carlisle (Kingmoor) on 16th June 1963, a depot it had been at since May 1961. For much of its working life it worked from 11C Oxenholme assisting trains up the incline to Grayrigg. Despite looking in fine fettle it was withdrawn from Kingmoor in October 1963. Backing up No 42301 is an unidentified LMS Class 4 2-6-0 'Flying Pig'. (N.E.Preedy)

144) We part company with the English side of the border with this final photograph of Kingmoor shed. LMS *Coronation* Class 4-6-2 No 46255 *City of Hereford,* a local engine, poses in the shed yard on 16th June 1963. Behind *City of Hereford* is a member of the LMS Class 4F 0-6-0's. Observe the strange looking device half-way up the water column which appears to be a brazier of some description. (N.E.Preedy)

145) After having crossed the England/Scotland border at the River Sark we depart from Cumberland and travel into Dumfries-shire, stopping for a brief sojourn at Dumfries itself. A plethora of tracks are straddled by a boarded crossing in front of which is an immaculate LMS *Jubilee* Class 4-6-0 No 45588 *Kashmir,* from 12A Carlisle (Kingmoor), on 15th April 1963. (B.Rands)

146) Dumfries used to be a junction for lines to Lockerbie and Stranraer, but nowadays it is simply a stopping point on the line from Carlisle to Glasgow. Former McIntosh Caledonian Class 3F 0-6-0 No 57572 (67B Hurlford) labours through Dumfries station with a mixed freight train on 18th August 1962. Despite the ever increasing number of diesels becoming available No 57572 managed to survive until June 1963. (J.Schatz)

147) For some strange reason the Scottish Region appeared to adopt a policy of cleaning the engine section of LMS Class 2P 4-4-0's, but not their tenders. Why this happened no-one seems to know. Because of this, No 40576, a local engine, looks rather odd in its home surroundings at 68B Dumfries on 27th June 1959. Despite looking in fine fettle it was taken out of traffic five months later and scrapped at Cowlairs Works. (A.N.H.Glover)

148) A member of the footplate crew of McIntosh Caledonian Railway 'Dunalastair' Class IV (3P) 4-4-0 No 54443 chats to a colleague inside the cab of the engine as it is prepared for a local passenger working in the shed yard at Dumfries on 2nd June 1950. Constructed in 1911 this Dumfries loco was declared surplus to traffic requirements in November 1955. (T.B.Owen)

149) A selection of former Caledonian locomotives on show in the shed yard at Dumfries on 14th June 1959, include an unidentified Class 3F 0-6-0 with a stovepipe chimney. Nearest the camera, with a lipped funnel, is locally based Pickersgill Caledonian Class 3F 0-6-0 No 57623 without smokebox door handles, a wheel taking the place of the same. Dumfries shed closed its doors for ever on 22nd October 1966. (D.K.Jones)

150) Before we arrive at Kilmarnock there used to be a branch line to Darvel, which once extended to Strathaven and beyond. We briefly visit Darvel on 21st June 1960. LMS Class 2P 4-4-0 No 40686 (67B Hurlford) awaits departure with a three coach local for Kilmarnock. This former Glasgow and South Western Railway line closed in 1964 along with the intermediate stations at Barleith, Galston and Newmilns. (F.Hornby)

151) An almost pure Caledonian scene in terms of locomotive power in the yard adjacent to the running shed at 67B Hurlford, the depot for Kilmarnock on 21st June 1960. An inmate of the depot, large boilered Pickersgill Caledonian Class 3F 0-6-0 No 57650 awaits its next turn of duty. Numerically speaking No 57650 was the first member of the class, but by November 1961 it was rendered redundant from Hurlford. (F.Hornby)

152) Judging by the bedraggled state of former Caledonian Railway Class 2P 0-4-4T No 55264 it looks as if its life is over, being in a store line next to a large snowplough in the yard at 67B Hurlford on 16th May 1959. However, fate was soon to intervene and the following month it was back in steam prior to being despatched to a new home at 67A Corkerhill (Glasgow). (D.K.Jones)

153) At first glance it appears that two coal wagons in the background are 'parked piggy-back' on top of the boiler of out of use LMS Class 2P 4-4-0 No 40645 which is in store at 67B Hurlford on 21st May 1961, in company with two sister locomotives. Despite its storage No 40645 was not condemned until October 1961. It was not until March/April 1962 that it was removed for scrapping at Inverurie Works. (D.K.Jones)

154) Tracks, signals and a signalbox crowd the left hand side of this picture whilst the right hand side appears to be a wasteland of rusting rails and weeds. McIntosh Caledonian Class 2P 0-4-4T No 55211 (67B Hurlford) approaches the station with empty stock on 22nd June 1960. The line in the left of the frame disappears off to Barassie and Ayr. Built in 1911 No 55211 was condemned from Hurlford in September 1961. (F.Hornby)

155) Black smoke pours from the chimney of 67B Hurlford based LMS Class 2P 4-4-0 No 40570 as it steams into Kilmarnock station with a local passenger train on 1st June 1950. No 40570 looks in ex. works condition and presents a fine sight in its lined livery. Records show that it was still allocated to Hurlford in 1957, not being taken out of traffic until August 1961 - scrapped at Inverurie Works later in the year. (T.B.Owen)

156) Riddles Austerity WD Class 8F 2-10-0 No 90752, with a tractive effort of some 34,215 lbs, powers a lengthy mineral train at Kilmarnock on a through road on 5th June 1952. It has not as yet acquired its proper front numberplate, having a chalked number instead. Designed by the Ministry of Supply in 1943 this class of twenty-five units was purchased for BR in 1948. On the left is a Leeds to St.Enoch express (T.B.Owen)

157) The next location on our long journey is at Caldwell, between Kilmarnock and Barrhead, on the former Glasgow, Barrhead and Kilmarnock Joint line. LMS Class 2P 4-4-0 No 40686, from 67B Hurlford, heads for home with the 7.10 pm local passenger train from St.Enoch on 7th August 1954. Note the Caledonian Railway route indicator on the bufferbeam of No 40686. (Peter Hay)

158) Looking in a reverse direction on the same date sister locomotive No 40612, with painted smokebox hinges and number-plate, passes a double upper quadrant signal post and clatters over points whilst in charge of the 7.33 pm stopping train from Kilmarnock to St.Enoch. No 40612, withdrawn from Hurlford in October 1961, was cut up at the BR Carriage & Wagon Works at Heatheryknowe, Glasgow in January 1962. Caldwell station closed in 1966. (Peter Hay)

159) The next station along the line from Caldwell was at Neilston also of Glasgow, Barrhead & Kilmarnock vintage which again was the subject of closure during 1966. On 7th August 1954 LMS Class 4P 'Compound' 4-4-0 No 40913, from 67A Corkerhill (Glasgow), provides 'super power' for a short wheelbased empty milk coach bound for Dumfries from Glasgow. (Peter Hay)

160) An upper quadrant mounted on a massive Scottish style lattice- post guards the entrance into Neilston station as LMS Class 2P No 40618, from 67B with Hurlford painted on the bufferbeam, lays a trail of black smoke as it storms away from its stop and heads southwards with the 7.39 pm local to Kilmarnock on 8th August 1953. A transfer to the Aberdeen area in February 1957 took No 40618 well away from the west of Scotland. (Peter Hay)

161) As we approach Glasgow (St.Enoch) we reach the suburbs where the engines used in and out of this particular terminus were housed - at 67A Corkerhill, of Glasgow & South Western Railway design. Like many large depots it had a mixture of locomotive classes right down to the humblest tank types. In steam in the yard next to a hoist is one of its stud of Mackintosh Caledonian Class 2P 0-4-4 Tanks No 55235 on 27th August 1957. (N.L.Browne)

162) A batch of LMS *Jubilee* Class 4-6-0's were allocated to Corkerhill shed, but they never appeared to be popular with the authorities there in comparison to their English colleagues. One of their number, No 45720 *Indomitable* is wedged between a Caledonian 0-4-4T and an LMS Class 4P 'Compound' 4-4-0 in the yard out of steam on 17th May 1953. Built at Crewe Works in 1936 it was withdrawn from Corkerhill in December 1962. (F.Hornby)

163) In its latter days as a working steam depot Corkerhill received quite a large number of BR Standard types, including the Class 4 2-6-4 Tanks for use on suburban services in and out of St.Enoch. Parked outside the running shed on 8th August 1965 is Class 4 2-6-4T No 80025 and BR Class 5 4-6-0 No 73098, a visitor to Corkerhill from 66A Polmadie (Glasgow) on 8th August 1965. (J.M.Tolson)

164) A grey and drab day at Corkerhill shed on 15th June 1958. Parked beneath the hoist on this date in time is LMR Class 2P 4-4-0 No 40598, a local engine. To the rear of No 40598 is another Corkerhill locomotive BR Class 4 2-6-4T No 80008. In the right of the picture is an unidentified LMS Class 4 2-6-4T. Withdrawn from Corkerhill in November 1959, No 40598 was scrapped at McLellans, Langloan in February 1960. (N.L.Browne)

165) Corkerhill station is in the left background as the footplate crew of McIntosh Caledonian Class 2P 4-4-0 No 55225, a long established member of the shed, pose for the camera on 27th August 1957 as it is about to depart after having a lamp affixed to a lamp iron. No 55225, condemned from Corkerhill in January 1962, was not cut up until September 1963. 67A ceased its long association with steam on 1st May 1967. (N.L.Browne)

166) We finally arrive at Glasgow (St.Enoch) after a long and winding journey from London. As can be seen the tracks into this station come in off a severe curve. A Sharp-Stewart built (1900) '856' Class McIntosh Caledonian 3F 0-6-0 No 57594, from 67A Corkerhill, is acting as a station pilot on 8th August 1953. No 57594 left Corkerhill in October 1957 for pastures new at 60A Inverness where it remained until April 1962. (Peter Hay)

67) There is an air of dereliction around the terminus in September 1961 as if the cloud of closure was on the horizon, with the building on the left having lost most of its windows. The driver of BR Class 2 2-6-0 No 77019, from 67B Hurlford, looks from the cab of his charge as it travels along light engine. No 77019, the last member of the class, had a short spell at 66A Polmadie in 1963 before returning once more to Hurlford. (G.W.Sharpe)

68) Unlike the closed in confines at Glasgow (Central) and Queen Street, St.Enoch was a light and airy place with wide plat-forms. A rake of vintage coaches are marshalled behind LMS Class 2P 4-4-0 No 40624 which awaits departure to Ardrossan with a semi- fast passenger train on 8th August 1953. This engine demised from 67D Ardrossan in August 1961, being cut up at Cowlairs Works in October 1962. (Peter Hay)

169) The huge overall roof structure at St.Enoch hides much of the inside of the station on a drab and miserable day in January 1963. LMS Class 5 4-6-0 No 45251, from 67D Ardrossan, waits to leave with an express bound for the west coast of Scotland. No 45251 is hemmed in by diesel multiple units - soon destined to take over most passenger services from St.Enoch. (G.W.Sharpe)

170) From a Caledonian Railway Class first introduced into service in 1910, 3P 4-4-0 No 54440, a 66D Greenock (Ladyburn) locomotive, shows off its lined livery as it accelerates a local stopping train out of the terminus in the 1950's. Despite mass dieselisation of the services to and from Glasgow (St.Enoch), this once fine station felt the full force of the Beeching axe and closure came in 1966, and it became 'another' car park. (Peter Hay)